Education is not the filling of a pail, but the lighting of a fire. – William Butler Yeats

Dedication

To every child who dreams without boundaries.
To every parent who believes in nurturing potential over pressure.
And to every educator who teaches from the heart —

This book is for you.

Preface

Education today stands at an extraordinary crossroads.

We live in a time where information is abundant, but true learning is rare. Schools are expected not just to teach academics, but to prepare children for an unpredictable, complex future.

As a parent, choosing a school for your child can feel overwhelming — even paralyzing. Curriculum choices, teaching methods, school philosophies, peer environments, board exams — all these decisions impact not just academic outcomes, but your child's self-esteem, mental health, and long-term happiness.

Through my years of working closely with schools, Teachers and families across India and abroad, I realized there was a pressing need for a comprehensive, **practical**, and **honest** guide for parents navigating this complex terrain. A guide that doesn't just list options — but empowers you to make *the right choice for your unique child*.

In *Selecting a School!* I combine research, real-life narratives, psychometric insights, and global educational wisdom to support you on this critical journey.

Whether your child is a toddler, a middle grader, or about to enter high school — this book will meet you where you are.

Remember:

**You are not just selecting a school.
You are shaping a life.**

Because selecting a school is not about fitting into a system — it's about discovering a path where our child can blossom.

I invite you to read this book not just with your mind, but with your heart wide open.

- **Vinothkumar Subramanian**

Index

- **Introduction:** The First Big Decision

- **Chapter 1:** The Indian School Landscape – A Brief History and the Birth of Macaulay's System

- **Chapter 2:** Understanding Montessori – Learning with Freedom and Discipline

- **Chapter 3:** Waldorf/Steiner Education – Learning Through Head, Heart, and Hands

- **Chapter 4:** Jiddu Krishnamurti's Vision – Awakening Intelligence, Not Conditioning

- **Chapter 5:** Understanding Indian School Boards – CBSE, ICSE, IGCSE, IB & More

- **Chapter 6:** Exams, Transitions & Report Cards – What They Really Say About Your Child

- **Chapter 7:** Beyond Syllabus – Teachers, School Leadership & Culture

- **Chapter 8:** Myths & Misconceptions about Modern Education

- **Chapter 9:** Transitioning from Traditional to Alternative Schooling

- **Chapter 10:** The Role of Parents in Education Today

- **Chapter 11:** Exploring the Future of Education

- **Chapter 12:** Making the Right Choice – Selecting the Best School for Your Child

Introduction: The First Big Decision

If you're holding this book in your hand, chances are, you're a parent standing at the threshold of one of the most important decisions you'll ever make — choosing the right school for your child. It's a decision that often comes with sleepless nights, endless WhatsApp forwards, unsolicited advice, school visits, and many, many Google searches.

But here's the truth — there's no "one best school" out there.

The best school is the one that **resonates with your child's learning style**, aligns with your family's values, and prepares your child for life — not just exams.

In India, the educational landscape is a complex blend of traditions, philosophies, boards, methods, reforms, and contradictions. From legacy institutions shaped by Lord Macaulay's colonial visions to child-centred environments inspired by Maria Montessori or Jiddu Krishnamurti, the diversity is immense — and overwhelming. Add to this the alphabet soup of boards: CBSE, ICSE, IGCSE, IB, NIOS — and you're left wondering whether you're selecting a school or decoding a cryptic puzzle.

Why This Book?

As an author, educator, and someone who has walked through school corridors in every role — student, teacher, principal, and parent — I wrote this book to bring **clarity** to this crucial process. This is not a ranking of schools, nor an endorsement of one board over the other. It's a **comprehensive guide** — grounded in experience, peppered with stories, and written with empathy.

Whether you are a first-time parent, someone relocating cities, or a family considering a shift from mainstream to alternative education — this book is for you.

What This Book Covers:

- The different **types of schools** in India and the educational philosophies they follow — including Macaulay's colonial system, Montessori, Waldorf/Steiner, Krishnamurti schools (KFI), and more.

- The **teaching methods** used in each system and how they shape your child's thinking, creativity, and self-confidence.

- A breakdown of **major boards** (CBSE, ICSE, IGCSE, IB, NIOS), with real-life examples of what children gain — and lose — in each.

- Clear, comparative insights into **exam patterns**, **report cards**, **assessment styles**, and how each system evaluates success.

- Narratives and case studies of children who thrived — and those who struggled — so that we move beyond theory and step into reality.

Choosing with Awareness

Our children are not blank slates. They are born with their own temperaments, passions, and learning styles. The question we need to ask is not "Which school is the best?" but **"Which school brings out the best in my child?"**

And that's what this book hopes to help you answer.

Each chapter is designed to gently walk you through this journey — with facts, questions, stories, and checklists — so you can choose not from fear or peer pressure, but from **informed confidence.**

Let's begin this journey together.

Because every child deserves an education that fits like a glove, not a uniform.

Chapter 1:

The Indian School Landscape

– A Brief History and the Birth of Macaulay's System

"True education must speak the language of freedom, not the echoes of colonization."
– Vinothkumar Subramanian

The Roots of Modern Schooling in India

Before the era of uniforms, report cards, and school buses, India had a very different relationship with learning. Education was deeply embedded in the community — through *Gurukuls*, *Madrasas*, *Pathshalas*, and home-based mentorship. Learning was flexible, personalized, and often deeply philosophical. Children learned astronomy, agriculture, mathematics, medicine, languages, and ethics — not through textbooks, but through lived experiences and oral tradition.

This system, however, began to shift dramatically during the colonial era, particularly with the arrival of **Lord Thomas Babington Macaulay**, who is often credited (or blamed) for laying the foundation of modern schooling in India.

Macaulay's Minute – A Turning Point

In 1835, Macaulay delivered his now-infamous "Minute on Indian Education." His goal was simple — to create a class of Indians who would be, in his own words, ***"Indian in blood and colour, but English in taste, in opinions, in morals, and in intellect."***

Macaulay believed that traditional Indian education was "worthless" and "barbaric" and proposed a new system that would focus on the **English language**, **Western literature**, and a curriculum that produced **clerks**, **interpreters**, and **administrators** for the British Empire.

And so began the birth of what we now call the **mainstream Indian schooling system** — structured, hierarchical, exam-oriented, and deeply influenced by **colonial values**.

What Did Macaulay's Model Look Like?

Let's break it down:

- **Language Shift**: English became the dominant medium of instruction, pushing classical Indian languages and local dialects to the background.

- **Content Shift**: Indian history, science, philosophy, and culture were replaced by British literature, Western science, and Christian ethics.

- **Pedagogy Shift**: The focus moved from dialogue and reflection to rote memorization, standardization, and regurgitation of facts.

- **Purpose Shift**: Education was no longer about self-realization or societal contribution — it was about passing exams and qualifying for government jobs.

Over the next century, this system became deeply entrenched, even after India's independence. The irony? A model designed to serve the British Empire still defines how millions of Indian children are educated today.

Legacy and Influence

Even now, most conventional schools in India — especially those following CBSE or State Board curricula — continue to reflect the **Macaulay template**. The emphasis remains on:

- **Textbook learning**

- **Standardized testing**

- **One-size-fits-all teaching**

- **Authority-driven classrooms**

Children are expected to sit still, listen, remember, and repeat. Curiosity is often curbed in favour of syllabus completion. Assessment is usually in the form of a final exam, and a student's "worth" is measured by marks, not by creativity, collaboration, or critical thinking.

Why This Matters for Parents Today

Many Indian parents today unconsciously associate "quality education" with the same rigid structures Macaulay introduced — uniforms, exams, English-speaking ability, and 90%+ scores.

But the world our children are growing into is vastly different from the world Macaulay designed his system for.

- Jobs are no longer limited to clerical or administrative roles.

- Skills like **communication, innovation, problem-solving, emotional intelligence, and adaptability** are more important than memorizing facts.

- Global education systems are shifting towards **child-centric**, **skills-based**, and **values-driven** learning models.

This brings us to a crucial question:

Is the Schooling Model You're Choosing Still Stuck in 1835?

Understanding Macaulay's influence is not about rejecting traditional schooling outright — it's about becoming aware. It's about realizing that what we call "normal" schooling today was never built with the child in mind — it was built with the colonization in mind.

In 1854, Charles Wood's Despatch shaped Indian education to create clerks, not thinkers — focusing on English for communication, math for calculation, and science for operation, not innovation.

And that's where alternative systems like **Montessori**, **Waldorf**, **Steiner**, and **Krishnamurti education** step in — systems that were **designed for the child**, not for the clerk.

Real-Life Story: The 90% Illusion

Vikram, a 10-year-old in Chennai, scored 94% in his final exams. His parents beamed with pride. But when they moved to Singapore and enrolled him in a school with project-based learning and presentations, Vikram froze. He had never been asked for his opinion in class. He could memorize and write, but he couldn't speak, present, or think out loud.

His Singapore teacher noted, "He's smart, but he's scared of making mistakes. He waits for someone to tell him what to do."

This is the unspoken cost of a system built on obedience over curiosity.

What's Coming Up

In the next chapters, we'll dive into the philosophies that offer a different path — from **Montessori** to **Waldorf** to **Krishnamurti's schools**. Each system has its own strengths and limitations, but they all share one thing in common:

They were built for the child's growth — not the government's convenience.

Let's explore these paths with open eyes and an open heart.

Chapter 2:
Understanding Montessori
– Learning with Freedom and Discipline

"Freedom and discipline are not opposites — they are the wings on which true learning soars."

– Dr.Maria Montessori

The Montessori Revolution

When Dr. Maria Montessori opened her first classroom — *Casa dei Bambini* (Children's House) — in Rome in 1907, she wasn't trying to build a new education system. She was responding to a simple question: **"What happens when children are trusted, respected, and allowed to learn at their own pace?"**

What she discovered transformed the world of education.

Today, over 22,000 Montessori schools exist globally — from Italy to India, from forest villages to Silicon Valley. Some of the most innovative minds — including **Google founders Larry Page and Sergey Brin**, **Amazon's Jeff Bezos**, and even **NBA player Stephen Curry** — have credited Montessori with shaping their thinking and creativity.

But what exactly is Montessori education? And how is it different from the conventional system most of us grew up in?

Core Philosophy: Follow the Child

Montessori education is built on one radical idea:

Children are naturally curious and capable of driving their own learning.

Instead of forcing all children to learn the same thing at the same time, Montessori respects each child's **individual pace**, **interests**, and **developmental rhythm**.

The teacher is not the centre of the classroom — the **child is**.

Key Features of Montessori Education

Let's break it down:

1. Prepared Environment

Montessori classrooms are calm, inviting, and designed for **independent exploration**. Every shelf and material have a purpose. Children can move freely, choose their work, and return it when done. This environment encourages **order**, **concentration**, and **choice**.

2. Hands-On Learning Materials

Instead of textbooks and blackboards, children learn with beautiful, tactile materials — from bead chains for math to sandpaper letters for phonics. These materials are **self-correcting**, allowing children to spot and fix their own mistakes without adult intervention.

3. Mixed-Age Classrooms

Children of **three-year age spans** learn together — for example, 3–6 years, 6–9 years, and so on. This fosters **peer learning**, **mentorship**, and a non-competitive atmosphere.

4. No Exams or Report Cards

Assessment in Montessori is **observational and continuous**. Teachers maintain detailed notes on each child's progress — not to rank them, but to support their growth. There are no marks, no grades — just feedback and reflection.

5. Freedom within Limits

Children are free to choose their work, but within **clear boundaries**. They learn to manage time, take responsibility, and respect others' space. This balance builds both **freedom** and **discipline** — a Montessori trademark.

Montessori in India – A Quiet Movement

India has a strong and growing Montessori presence, especially in pre-primary education. Cities like Chennai, Bengaluru, and Pune have well-established Montessori schools. Some even extend to **elementary and adolescent levels**, though these are still fewer in number.

A few Indian pioneers, like **Rukmini Ramachandran**, have worked tirelessly to bring authentic Montessori practices to Indian classrooms, blending global philosophy with local culture.

Real-Life Story: Aarav's Transformation

Aarav, a 5-year-old from Coimbatore, was withdrawn and labelled as "slow" in his previous preschool. His parents were told he had "attention issues." They shifted him to a Montessori environment on a trial basis.

Within three months, Aarav was sweeping the classroom floor, arranging flowers, learning math with beads, and — most importantly — smiling. His teachers observed that **he wasn't slow; he just needed space and time.**

Three years later, Aarav now confidently helps younger children tie their shoelaces and reads simple Tamil and English books. No labels. No shame. Just growth.

Is Montessori Right for Your Child?

Let's look at some **benefits** and **challenges** of the Montessori system.

✅ **Benefits:**

- Builds **confidence**, **concentration**, and **independence**

- Fosters a **love for learning**, not just information gathering

- Promotes **intrinsic motivation** instead of reward-punishment cycles

- Supports **emotional and social development**

- Adapts to **each child's pace** — ideal for both fast and slow learners

⚠️ **Challenges:**

- Requires **trained Montessori adults** — not just any teacher

- Can be **misused by schools** using the "Montessori" label without authenticity

- May not suit families who prefer frequent testing, competition, or conventional grading

Montessori vs Conventional: A Quick Glance

Feature	Montessori	Conventional
Curriculum	Child-led, interest-based	Fixed syllabus, teacher-led
Classroom	Mixed-age, open movement	Same-age, fixed desks
Materials	Hands-on, self-correcting	Textbooks, worksheets
Assessment	Continuous observation	Exams, grades, report cards
Media Use	No screens till age 12+	Screen-based smart classes common
Motivation	Internal (love for work)	External (marks, praise, punishment)

A Note for Parents

Choosing Montessori is not just about choosing a school — it's about embracing a **philosophy of parenting**. One that values **respect**, **trust**, and **freedom** over fear, control, and comparison.

If your child is naturally curious, loves hands-on work, or struggles with rigid environments, Montessori could be a wonderful fit. But remember, no system is perfect. What matters is alignment — between your child, your parenting beliefs, and the school's values.

Coming Up Next

In the next chapter, we'll explore another alternative: the **Waldorf/Steiner approach**, which blends art, imagination, and holistic development into a soulful education journey.

Chapter 3:

Waldorf/Steiner Education
– Learning Through Head, Heart, and Hands

"The hands that paint and craft are the same hands that one day shape the world."

- Rudolf Steiner

The Soul of Waldorf Education

Imagine a school where children paint before they read, learn mathematics through movement, and spend their early years immersed in storytelling, handcrafts, and nature.

That's not a fantasy — it's the reality of a Waldorf school.

Founded in 1919 by **Rudolf Steiner**, an Austrian philosopher and visionary, the Waldorf (also called Steiner) education system believes that **education is not just to inform the mind, but to nourish the soul**.

Steiner saw each child as a unique being on a lifelong journey of growth. His schools were designed to support **intellectual, emotional, and spiritual development** — what he called the "head, heart, and hands" approach.

The Waldorf Philosophy: Rhythm, Imagination, Wholeness

At the heart of Waldorf education is a deep respect for the **developmental stages of childhood**. Steiner believed that education should not rush the child but instead align with their natural unfolding — much like a flower blooming in its own time.

Waldorf classrooms feel almost magical — no digital screens, no fluorescent lights, no rote learning. Instead, you'll find **storytelling, poetry recitation, gardening, sculpting, knitting, movement**, and songs.

It's an education that **slows down time** in the best possible way.

Key Features of Waldorf Education

1. Delayed Academics

In most Waldorf schools, children are introduced to reading, writing, and math only around age **7** — not because they're slow, but because early childhood is seen as a sacred phase for **imagination, movement, and play**.

2. Storytelling and Art as Core Learning Tools

Rather than textbooks, teachers narrate **epic stories**, **folk tales**, **myths**, and **legends** from around the world. Children illustrate what they learn in **Main Lesson Books**, which become personalized textbooks.

3. The Same Teacher for Years

From Grade 1 to Grade 8, the **same teacher** stays with the class, forming deep, meaningful bonds with the students. This continuity fosters emotional security and personalized understanding.

4. No Exams, No Competition

Like Montessori, Waldorf schools don't rely on tests or grades. The emphasis is on **progress**, not performance. **Narrative report cards** provide rich, descriptive feedback instead of marks.

5. Art, Movement, and Craft Integrated Daily

From **Eurythmy** (a movement-based art form unique to Waldorf) to knitting and woodworking, children experience learning not just with the mind, but through the body and hands. Every subject is artistic in delivery — even math is painted!

Waldorf in India – A Quietly Growing Network

Though not as widespread as Montessori, Waldorf schools are steadily growing in India. Cities like **Hyderabad, Bengaluru, Mumbai, Auroville**, and **Pune** host some of the most authentic Steiner schools.

These schools attract parents looking for a **holistic, peaceful, and art-integrated education**, especially for young children. Many Indian Waldorf schools also integrate **local culture**, **festivals**, and **languages** with Steiner's European framework.

Real-Life Story: Leela's Waldorf Journey

Leela was a curious and sensitive child who disliked noisy classrooms and was easily overwhelmed by fast-paced academics. Her parents enrolled her in a Waldorf school in Hyderabad.

There, Leela painted math lessons, sang her science, acted out history, and learned gardening. At age 10, she had no formal exams under her belt — but could explain Indian epics with deep empathy, sew her own soft toy, and recite poetry fluently in English and Telugu.

Her mother says,

"Waldorf gave her the freedom to be a child. It protected her wonder — something I wish I had growing up."

Benefits and Challenges of Waldorf Education

☑ **Benefits**

- Deep focus on **imagination**, **creativity**, and **emotional health**

- Encourages **inner motivation** and **self-awareness**

- Strong connection between **teacher and child**

- Fosters **artistic and aesthetic sensitivity**

- Minimizes pressure and comparison

⚠ Challenges

- **Delayed academics** may feel risky to some parents

- Lack of **standardized exams** can complicate transitions to traditional systems

- Finding **certified Waldorf-trained teachers** in India is still a challenge

- Waldorf philosophy may not align with highly competitive academic goals (e.g., early Olympiads, entrance coaching, etc.)

Waldorf vs. Traditional Education: At a Glance

Feature	Waldorf	Conventional
Academics Start	Age 7	Age 4–5
Curriculum Style	Arts-integrated, story-based	Syllabus-focused, textbook-based
Teacher Role	Same teacher for years, facilitator	Grade-specific, subject teachers
Assessment	Narrative reports, no exams	Exams, grades, report cards
Media Use	No screens till age 12+	Screen-based smart classes common
Focus	Imagination, rhythm, holistic growth	Information delivery, academic performance

Is Waldorf Right for Your Family?

Waldorf education is a **lifestyle**, not just a school choice. It values **simplicity, nature, rhythm, and slow living**. If your family values storytelling over screen time, craft over competition, and emotional depth over early academic pressure, Waldorf might be a deeply fulfilling path.

However, if your long-term goals include **competitive exams, early acceleration, or structured assessments**, this system may feel misaligned unless planned thoughtfully.

Waldorf thrives best when home and school share similar values.

In Summary

Waldorf education brings **soul and imagination** into the heart of learning. It's not a system for rushing or measuring children but for letting them bloom in their own time, with reverence, rhythm, and joy.

Coming Up Next

In the next chapter, we'll explore an Indian-born, deeply spiritual approach to education — the **Krishnamurti Foundation schools**. Let's understand how these schools use silence, dialogue, and freedom to awaken consciousness in children.

Chapter 4:

Jiddu Krishnamurti's Vision – Awakening Intelligence, Not Conditioning

"The highest purpose of education is to free the mind, not fill it."

- J. Krishnamurti

An Education Rooted in Freedom and Awareness

"Real learning comes when the competitive spirit has ceased." – *Jiddu Krishnamurti*

In the bustling landscape of Indian education — where grades, competition, and rigid systems dominate — a quiet revolution exists. It does not shout for attention. It does not advertise rankings. Yet, it has quietly shaped some of the most thoughtful, free-thinking individuals in India.

We're speaking of the **Krishnamurti Foundation of India (KFI) schools** — institutions founded on the ideas of **Jiddu Krishnamurti**, a philosopher, speaker, and educator who believed that **education should awaken intelligence, not just accumulate knowledge**.

Who Was Jiddu Krishnamurti?

Born in **1895 in Madanapalle, Andhra Pradesh**, Krishnamurti was identified by the Theosophical Society as a future "World Teacher." However, in a historic moment of integrity, he **rejected all religious and political authority**, dissolved the Order formed in his name, and walked away from fame — choosing instead to **explore truth freely**, without dogma.

He spent his life speaking across the world, questioning everything from religion to nationalism, from fear to education.

At the heart of his philosophy was a simple but profound question:

Can education help a human being be inwardly free?

The KFI Schools: Not Just Another Curriculum

There are around **6 KFI schools** in India, located in **Bengaluru (Valley School), Chennai (The School), Varanasi (Rajghat Besant School), Uttarkashi (Himalaya Public School), Rishi Valley (a related school), and Sahyadri School near Pune**.

These are not alternative schools in the trendy sense — they are schools built on the foundation of **deep observation, dialogue, nature, and self-inquiry**.

Here, education is not preparation for a job — it's preparation for **life**. A full life, rich with awareness, empathy, and understanding of the self and the world.

Key Principles of KFI Education

1. Freedom from Fear and Comparison

KFI schools reject **reward-punishment psychology**, ranking systems, and academic pressure. Children are not labeled as "topper" or "average." Instead, they're encouraged to **explore, question, reflect, and observe**.

2. Learning Through Dialogue

Krishnamurti emphasized that learning happens in **conversation, not control**. Children regularly engage in **group dialogues**, exploring questions like:

- What is freedom?

- Why do we get angry?

- What is the role of thought?

These are not theoretical debates but deep reflections that **build awareness and sensitivity**.

3. Integration with Nature

Most KFI schools are located in **natural, non-urban settings**. Trees, birds, silence, and space are part of the classroom. This fosters a **sense of humility**, deep observation, and connection to the environment.

4. Teacher as Facilitator, Not Authority

Teachers are not enforcers — they are **co-learners**. The relationship is built on **respect and mutual exploration**. Krishnamurti called this the foundation of right relationship in education.

5. No Standardized Pressure

There is no rush for early academics, no standard exams in lower grades, and no obsession with board results. Yet, students from these schools do appear for **ICSE, ISC, or IGCSE** in higher classes, and they often excel — not through cramming, but clarity.

Real-Life Story: Aarav from Valley School

Aarav, now a 20-year-old social entrepreneur, grew up in a mainstream school until Class 5. The environment drained his curiosity. When his parents shifted him to the **Valley School, Bengaluru**, things changed.

He remembers:

"There were no school bells. The teacher asked us how we *felt* before starting math. We sat under a banyan tree to discuss fear — not solve equations. It blew my mind."

Today, Aarav leads a rural education NGO. He credits his journey to the **inner confidence and clarity** the Krishnamurti school nurtured in him.

KFI vs Traditional Schooling – What's the Difference?

Feature	KFI Schools	Traditional Schools
Learning Method	Inquiry-based, dialogue-driven	Textbook + lecture-based
Competition	None	High
Exams	Minimal, child-paced	Frequent, high-pressure
Teacher Role	Facilitator, co-learner	Authority figure
Curriculum	Flexible, ICSE/IGCSE later	Fixed and test-oriented
Focus	Awareness, observation, compassion	Academic achievement

Benefits of Krishnamurti Education

☑ **Encourages clarity of thought, not just content**
☑ Builds emotionally grounded, self-aware individuals
☑ Offers freedom without chaos — a sense of deep responsibility
☑ Equally rigorous in academics when the time is right
☑ Supports inner discipline, not imposed discipline

Challenges for Parents to Consider

⚠ **Hard to "measure" progress in early years**
⚠ May not suit families seeking early academic competition
⚠ Entry into KFI schools is limited and selective
⚠ Requires parental alignment with the school's values

These schools aren't looking to build the next CEO — they're looking to raise the **next generation of wise, awake, and compassionate human beings**.

Is a KFI School Right for Your Child?

If you believe that **education is not just about survival but about understanding life**, if your child is curious, sensitive, and thoughtful, and if you are willing to walk the path **with awareness and patience**, a Krishnamurti school might be your answer.

But be prepared: this is not a quick fix or shortcut. It is a journey — subtle, quiet, and inward.

In Summary

Krishnamurti's vision of education offers an alternative not just to curriculum, but to **the entire idea of what it means to learn**. His schools don't produce students — they nurture **observers, listeners, thinkers, and human beings who care**.

They remind us of what we often forget:

"It is no measure of health to be well-adjusted to a profoundly sick society." – *Krishnamurti*

Next Chapter Preview

In Chapter 5, we'll move into a practical comparison of **school boards in India** — from CBSE to IB to NIOS — and help parents navigate which board might align best with their child's personality and family's values.

Chapter 5:

Understanding Indian School Boards

– CBSE, ICSE, IGCSE, IB & More

"It's not about choosing the best board — it's about choosing the right journey for your child's soul."

– Vinothkumar Subramanian

Why School Boards Matter More Than We Think

When parents think of selecting a school, the first question is usually *"Which board is best?"* But the real question should be,

"Which board suits my child's learning style, temperament, and future goals?"

In India, school boards are not just administrative labels — they shape how your child learns, what they learn, how they're assessed, and in many cases, how they view education itself.

Let's explore the major boards in India and internationally available in India, and understand the **teaching methodologies, curriculum styles, exam patterns, and report card philosophies** behind each.

1. CBSE – Central Board of Secondary Education

Reach: Largest board in India, followed in both public and private schools.
Curriculum: Structured and theory oriented. Focus on Science, Maths, and Languages.

Teaching Style:

- Traditional classroom teaching

- Strong emphasis on *textbooks prescribed by NCERT*

- Encourages rote memorization in lower classes but gradually shifting towards *conceptual clarity*

Assessment:

- Uniform assessments across affiliated schools

- Recently introduced *CCE (Continuous Comprehensive Evaluation)* methods, but implementation varies

- Board exams at Class 10 and 12 level

Advantages:

☑ Recognized nationwide and preferred for national entrance exams (NEET, JEE)
☑ Easier school transfers across India
☑ Emphasizes core academic skills

Limitations:

⚠ Less emphasis on arts, creativity, or interdisciplinary learning
⚠ Heavy syllabus and exam pressure from Class 9 onward
⚠ Lacks flexibility in teaching approach

2. ICSE / ISC – Council for the Indian School Certificate Examinations

Reach: Popular in many elite urban schools.
Curriculum: Language-heavy, with strong emphasis on English, humanities, and diverse electives.

Teaching Style:

- Encourages project work, lab work, essays, and group discussions

- Textbooks are not centrally prescribed – schools can choose from approved publishers

- Balanced mix of theoretical and practical learning

Assessment:

- Exams in Class 10 (ICSE) and Class 12 (ISC)

- Internal assessments and projects carry significant weight

Advantages:

- ☑ Excellent language skills, especially English
- ☑ Encourages analytical thinking and depth
- ☑ Broad subject choices including music, art, environmental science

Limitations:

- ⚠ Comparatively vast syllabus
- ⚠ Slightly more academic pressure in higher classes
- ⚠ Not ideal for students aiming only for technical/engineering careers

3. IGCSE – International General Certificate of Secondary Education (UK-based)

Reach: Offered in many international schools in metros and Tier-1 cities.

Curriculum: Global curriculum developed by Cambridge (CAIE), designed for students aged 14–16.

Teaching Style:

- Skill-based, learner-centred, inquiry-driven

- No rigid textbooks; encourages wide reading and critical thinking

- Assessments include coursework, oral tests, presentations

Assessment:

- Students take exams in selected subjects (70+ options)

- Graded on an A* to G scale

- Encourages real-world application and logical thinking

Advantages:

☑ Globally recognized
☑ Excellent foundation for international higher education
☑ Flexible subject combinations

Limitations:

⚠ High cost of schooling and exams
⚠ Limited availability in small towns
⚠ Additional focus required for Indian competitive exams (JEE/NEET)

4. IB – International Baccalaureate (Swiss-based)

Programs: PYP (Primary Years), MYP (Middle Years), DP (Diploma), CP (Career-related).

Reach: Offered in premium international schools in India's major cities.

Teaching Style:

- Inquiry-led, research-based learning
- Focus on developing the "whole child" – intellectually, emotionally, ethically
- No fixed textbooks; encourages independent exploration

Assessment:

- Internal assessments, presentations, essays, projects
- External IB Diploma exams are known for academic rigor

Advantages:

☑ Globally respected and accepted by top universities
☑ Emphasis on critical thinking, communication, research skills
☑ Bilingual options, TOK (Theory of Knowledge), EE (Extended Essay) foster holistic learning

Limitations:

⚠ Extremely expensive
⚠ Demanding for average learners if not supported
⚠ Limited availability and difficult to switch from/to Indian boards

5. NIOS – National Institute of Open Schooling

Reach: Ideal for flexible, alternative education. Offered by the Indian government.
Curriculum: Similar to CBSE in subject offering, but far more flexible.

Teaching Style:

- Student-paced, often used for home-schooling or non-traditional learners
- Learners can choose subjects, take exams in their own timeline
- Available in many languages

Assessment:

- On-demand exams, practical's, assignments
- No strict academic calendar

Advantages:

☑ Ideal for special needs learners or athletes/artists/Alternative Schools like Montessori, Waldorf, KFI children who wish to pursue Indian Board exams
☑ Less stress, highly adaptable
☑ Government-recognized and valid for all competitive exams

Limitations:

⚠ Parents may feel something different since its Named Open Schooling
⚠ Less practical test compared to IGCSE / IB

What Do Report Cards Look Like Across Boards?

- **CBSE:** Marks and grades, subject-wise breakdown

- **ICSE:** Marks with detailed subject comments

- **IGCSE/IB:** Predicted grades, final exam scores, often with remarks on skill development

- **NIOS:** Consolidated scores, certificates post each level

The **language and format of report cards** also reflect the values of the board — rigid and mark-centric vs. reflective and skill-based.

Real-Life Contrast: Arjun vs. Sanvi

- **Arjun**, a CBSE student, scores 95% but rarely expresses his thoughts openly. His school report card reflects academic excellence, but his teachers have never seen his poetry notebook.

- **Sanvi**, an IB student, may score 88% overall but has a detailed portfolio of community service, environmental work, and a 3,000-word research paper on gender equality in Indian folklore.

Which child is more prepared for life? That depends on what we value more — marks or meaning.

So...Which Board is the Best?

There's no one right answer. But here's a starting point:

If your priority is...	Consider
Competitive exams & national mobility	CBSE
Language skills, balance, urban careers	ICSE
Global exposure, flexible learning	IGCSE / IB
Personalized, low-pressure education	NIOS
Reflective, freedom-centred learning	KFI or Montessori with open board

In Summary

The board you choose is like the soil you plant your child's learning roots in. Choose wisely. Choose based on:

- Your child's temperament
- Your family values
- Long-term academic and life goals
- Your willingness to participate in the learning journey

Challenges Parents Face

Choosing Traditional may feel safe because it's familiar — but it can risk burnout in sensitive children.

Choosing Progressive may feel risky because it's unfamiliar — but it can unlock talents traditional systems overlook.

👉 **Tip:**
Look at the end goal.
Do you want your child to just 'score' — or to *think, feel, create, and solve*?

👉 **Another Tip:**
Look at the transition possibilities.
Some progressive schools (especially IB, IGCSE) still prepare students very well for college and careers, just in different ways.

Next Chapter Preview

In Chapter 6, we'll go deeper into the **exam patterns, grading systems, and transition challenges** — what happens when your child moves from ICSE to CBSE? Or from IB to Indian colleges?

We'll also explore how **report cards** reflect a school's hidden culture.

Chapter 6:

Exams, Transitions & Report Cards – What They Really Say About Your Child

"A child's worth is measured not in marks, but in moments of curiosity, courage, and growth."

– Vinothkumar Subramanian

Exams Are Not Just Tests—They Are Mirrors

Across India and globally, exams are more than a system of evaluation. They reflect the philosophy of the school, the priorities of the board, and sometimes—unfortunately—the anxiety of the parent.

But what do these exams really *measure*? Are they judging intelligence? Effort? Memory? Creativity? Or something else?

Let's decode what exams, transitions between boards, and report cards really mean in the Indian education context.

1. Exam Patterns Across Major Boards

Each board approaches assessments differently, based on its core ideology.

CBSE

- *Format:* Subjective + objective questions, long answers, emphasis on accuracy.

- *Frequency:* School-level exams in lower classes, board exams in Classes 10 and 12.

- *Focus:* Science and Math-heavy, right/wrong answers.

- *Impact:* High pressure in higher classes due to national exam stakes.

ICSE / ISC

- *Format:* Longer descriptive answers, essays, lab records, internal assessments.

- *Frequency:* Periodic assessments, project work, final boards in Classes 10 & 12.

- *Focus:* Deep language skills, wide subject range.

- *Impact:* Academically demanding, High pressure but well-rounded.

IGCSE / IB

- *Format:* Internal assessments, coursework, oral exams, practical's, portfolios.

- *Frequency:* Flexible exams spread over years (not just one-shot).

- *Focus:* Application, reflection, real-life problem-solving.

- *Impact:* Encourages independence and critical thinking but demands maturity.

NIOS

- *Format:* Self-paced, open book in some cases, practical + theoretical.

- *Frequency:* On-demand or scheduled exams.

- *Focus:* Accessibility, low stress.

- *Impact:* Perfect for non-traditional learners.

2. Transitioning Between Boards – Can It Be Smooth?

In reality, many children switch boards at different points:

- Due to a transfer or relocation.

- Because the parent realizes the initial choice doesn't match the child's learning style.

- Financial or accessibility reasons.

Let's explore common transitions and their challenges:

CBSE to ICSE

- **Challenge:** Language-rich curriculum may feel heavier.

- **Tip:** Focus on building writing and grammar skills to catch up.

ICSE to CBSE

- **Challenge:** The pace may feel faster; conceptual clarity might be missing in some areas.

- **Tip:** Embrace NCERT-style learning. Practice structured answers.

CBSE/ICSE to IGCSE

- **Challenge:** From textbook learning to exploratory learning can overwhelm.

- **Tip:** Encourage open-book projects at home, support creative thinking.

IGCSE/IB/NIOS to Indian Boards (especially in high school)

- **Challenge:** Rigid curriculum, lack of flexibility, rote learning.

- **Tip:** Prepare emotionally. Start focused tutoring early for JEE/NEET, if needed.

3. The Truth Behind Report Cards

Have you ever wondered why some report cards list only marks while others write half a page about your child?

Let's decode:

Board	Style of Report Card	What It Reveals
CBSE	Marks + grades	Focus on academic performance only.
ICSE	Marks + remarks	Academic + language skills get visibility.
IB	Descriptors + grades	Skill development, behaviour, teamwork, initiative.
IGCSE	Grades + coursework feedback	Reflective, with focus on subject understanding.
NIOS	Marks + certification	Emphasis on subject clearance, less qualitative feedback.

A report card, ultimately, is just a snapshot. It doesn't tell you who your child *really is*. But it does reflect what the school *sees* as valuable.

4. Parent Trap: Obsessing Over Marks

It's natural to care about scores. But here's the uncomfortable truth:

◆ Many children who top school exams struggle in college.
◆ Many who perform average in boards thrive in careers.
◆ Some children with "average" report cards have exceptional leadership, creativity, and empathy.

Real-life story:

Reya, a 14-year-old in IGCSE, consistently scored B and C grades. Her parents were concerned. But she was leading the school's social impact club, organizing fundraisers and mentoring younger students.
Her final school report read: *"Reya is a reflective learner, a quiet leader, and a consistent team builder. A valuable community presence."*

Would that appear in a CBSE report card? Possibly not. But does it matter for life success? Absolutely.

5. The Missing Piece: Self-Assessment and Student Voice

Some progressive schools (especially in IB, Waldorf, and Montessori-inspired systems) involve students in evaluating themselves.

This includes:

- Setting learning goals

- Writing reflections

- Presenting personal growth journals

Why is this powerful?

Because your child begins to own their learning journey—not just perform for marks.

If your school doesn't offer this, create a space at home:

- Weekly reflections ("What did I enjoy learning this week?")

- Goal setting ("Next month, I want to improve in...")

- Celebrating progress, not just achievement

Final Takeaways

☑ Don't judge your child only by grades.
☑ Understand what each exam pattern is really testing.
☑ Transitions between boards are manageable—with support.

☑ Use report cards as conversation starters, not final judgments.
☑ Include your child in the process of reflection and goal setting.

Parent Prompt: Ask Yourself

- What does my child's current report card *not* tell me?

- Do I know how my child feels about their own learning?

- Am I chasing marks... or meaning?

Next Chapter Preview

In **Chapter 7**, we explore:
👉 *The Role of Teachers, Leadership, and School Culture* – Because choosing a school is not just about infrastructure or syllabus, but about *people and purpose.*

Chapter 7:

Beyond Syllabus

– Teachers, School Leadership & Culture

"A great school teaches children not what to think, but how to think and feel deeply."

– Vinothkumar Subramanian

When we think about schools, our minds often go to curriculum, textbooks, and exams. But the heart of any school isn't just its syllabus—it's **people**. A school is only as good as its **teachers**, **leaders**, and the **values** it breathes every day.

In this chapter, we'll dive into the invisible (but essential) layer that defines whether your child *loves* learning or just *survives* school.

1. The Teacher Matters—A Lot

Ask any adult about their favourite teacher, and they will tell you a story—not about what was taught, but how it made them feel.

What makes a great teacher?

- ☑ Knows the subject, but more importantly, knows the **child**.
- ☑ Builds trust and listens without judgment.
- ☑ Adapts teaching to the learning style of each child.
- ☑ Makes learning joyful, not fearful.

Real-life story:

In a Montessori school in Bengaluru, 8-year-old **Advait** struggled with writing. But his teacher noticed he loved creating comic strips. Instead of pushing him into worksheets, she encouraged him to write dialogues for his drawings. Within 6 months, his confidence in language soared.

That's the power of a teacher who observes and adapts.

Questions to Ask When Choosing a School:

- Are the teachers trained in **child development**, not just subject knowledge?

- Do they receive **ongoing professional development**?

- Do they speak **about children with empathy**, or only in terms of marks?

2. The Invisible Influence: School Leadership

A school's leadership team sets the tone—often more than the teachers. The values, policies, and vision of the principal or founder quietly shape the child's experience.

Signs of Positive Leadership:

☑ Transparent communication with parents
☑ Openness to feedback and change
☑ Prioritizes child wellbeing alongside academics
☑ Builds a collaborative team culture among teachers

Real-life story:

A small progressive school in Tamil Nadu held monthly "Tea with the Principal" sessions, where 10 random parents were invited to share concerns and ideas. The result?

- Reduced parent anxiety

- Real-time improvements in systems

- A culture of *shared ownership* in education

You may never meet the school owner often—but their decisions will ripple into your child's life daily.

3. School Culture: What Are Children Really Absorbing?

Culture is *not* printed on a prospectus. It is felt in the corridors.

You'll know the culture of a school by:

- How teachers speak to children and each other

- What behaviour is praised, and what is ignored

- How mistakes are treated (punished or learned from)

- What diverse learners (shy, hyperactive, creative, struggling) are included

☑ A culture of respect → builds confident learners
☑ A culture of comparison → builds anxious performers
☑ A culture of curiosity → builds lifelong learners
☑ A culture of compliance → builds silent followers

Observe the school for 30 minutes on a regular day. The truth lies between the lines.

4. The Relationship Triangle: Child–Teacher–Parent

The most successful schools know this secret:

When the child, teacher, and parent are in harmony, growth becomes natural.

Let's break it down:

- **Teacher ↔ Child:** Trust and safety must be built. A child should feel they can express doubt or fear.

- **Parent ↔ Teacher:** Mutual respect and teamwork. Not blame or overdependence.

- **Parent ↔ Child:** Acceptance of effort, not just achievement. Letting the child take ownership.

Tip:

Before enrolling, ask:

- *How do you communicate with parents?*

- *Do you share regular feedback, or only during report cards?*

- *Are there parent workshops or involvement programs?*

A school that includes you—without overwhelming you—is the sweet spot.

5. Does the School Walk Its Talk?

Most schools promise "holistic learning," "21st-century skills," and "child-centred education." But not all walk that talk.

Here's how to test it:

Claim	Check for Evidence
"We nurture creativity"	Do children have time for art, drama, or unstructured play?
"We are child-centric"	Are assessments flexible? Are children given voice in learning?
"We value character"	Are empathy, teamwork, or kindness rewarded in any way?
"We prepare global citizens"	Is the curriculum culturally inclusive and globally aware?

Real-life example:

A school claimed to promote "growth mindset." But when a child failed a math test, the teacher wrote: "Disappointed. Needs to work harder." Contrast this with another school where the comment was: "Let's explore new strategies together next time. You've shown great persistence." Same marks—different mindset.

6. Trust Your Inner Compass

As a parent, you may visit several schools—some with huge campuses and perfect brochures. But listen to your *inner signal*.

Did the environment feel *joyful*? Did you see children who were *curious*? Did the teachers speak with *respect and warmth*?

A school building doesn't need to be perfect. But it must feel human.

Closing Thoughts

When choosing a school, don't just ask:

✕ "What syllabus do you follow?"
✕ "How many students score above 90%?"
✕ "Do you have smart boards and CCTV?"

Ask instead:

☑ "What values guide your teaching?"
☑ "How do you support children who learn differently?"
☑ "How do you nurture self-confidence?"

Because at the end of the day, schools are not factories. They are ecosystems of people, passion, and purpose.

Parent Prompt: Reflection Journal

"List 3 values you want your child to experience at school every day. Now check—does the school you're considering truly reflect those values?"

Next Chapter Preview: Chapter 8 – Myths & Misconceptions about Modern Education

Up next, we'll bust some big myths like:

- "Montessori is only for toddlers."

- "Children need pressure to succeed."

- "Alternative schools can't prepare kids for real life."

Chapter 8:

Myths & Misconceptions about Modern Education

"The future belongs to those who dare to question the myths of yesterday."

- Unknown

In every parent group, playground chat, or family WhatsApp group, you'll hear *opinions* about education—some helpful, many half-baked.

This chapter is here to gently bust some of the most common myths that confuse or worry parents when exploring alternative or modern schooling methods.

1. "Montessori is only for preschool."

One of the biggest myths around the Montessori method is that it's only for ages 2 to 6. In truth, Dr. Maria Montessori designed a complete system from birth through adolescence.

Montessori Elementary (ages 6–12) and even adolescent (ages 12–24) programs exist across the world. They focus on:

- **Big-picture thinking**
- **Cosmic education (interconnected learning)**
- **Real-world application**
- **Self-discipline, not imposed discipline**

✅ Myth busted: Montessori is a **complete educational philosophy**, not a pre-primary daycare trend.

Real-life: In Chennai, 15-year-old Tanvi who moved from a CBSE school to Montessori said, "Here, we don't just memorize. We figure out *why* things happen. Even history feels like a storybook."

2. "Children need pressure to succeed."

There's an old belief: *Without pressure, children will become lazy*. But current neuroscience says otherwise. Excess pressure triggers the stress response in the brain—blocking **curiosity**, **creativity**, and **intrinsic motivation**.

Healthy challenge? Yes. Constant stress and comparison? No.

✅ Modern education methods focus on **motivation from within**—not just fear of marks.

A school in Delhi replaced unit tests with open-ended projects and saw not only improved learning but also a **75% drop in student anxiety**.

3. "Alternative schools can't prepare kids for real life."

What is "real life"? If it means stress, deadlines, competition—yes, alternative schools may not simulate that.
But if real life means:

- Collaborating with others

- Solving real problems

- Managing time

- Thinking independently

Then these schools may be doing **a better job**.

✅ In fact, many alumni of Waldorf, KFI, Montessori combined IGCSE/NIOS/IB schools grow up to be

entrepreneurs, creators, global thinkers, and ethical leaders.

Story: A child from a Steiner school went on to become a successful product designer. In an interview, he said, "We were taught to imagine solutions before being shown models. That's how I now approach every design brief."

4. "If there's no homework or exams, kids won't learn."

Here's the truth: Homework and exams are tools. But *learning* can happen without them if the system is well designed.

- Instead of exams: Continuous observation, real-life projects, and skill-based assessments

- Instead of homework: Deep work done during school hours, allowing **free time at home for exploration and family bonding**

☑ Studies show that excessive homework in early years brings **no academic benefit** but does cause stress and family conflict.

Alternative schools focus on **quality of understanding**, not quantity of worksheets.

5. "All kids should follow the same path."

This myth stems from our own upbringing, where school, marks, college, and job were seen as a fixed sequence.

But the world your child will grow up in will reward:

- Flexibility

- Innovation

- Emotional intelligence

- Personal branding

One-size-fits-all schooling may not prepare children for a **multi-career, tech-enabled, passion-driven world**.

☑ The best schools today offer space for **customized growth paths**, not rigid templates.

6. "Marks are the only measure of success."

This belief has created generations of high-performing but **deeply insecure** adults.

Marks can reflect performance on a **specific day** under **specific conditions**. They are not a measure of:

- Curiosity

- Collaboration

- Resilience

- Passion

☑ Progressive schools report learning through **portfolios, projects, presentations**, and **self-reflection journals**—all offering a more accurate picture of a child's growth.

Real-life: In a Chennai school, students maintain personal learning journals where they reflect on weekly wins and challenges. A parent said, "It tells me more about my child than any report card ever did."

7. "Alternative schools lack discipline."

Another myth! The idea that only uniformity and punishment bring discipline is outdated.

True discipline is:

- Self-directed

- Rooted in internal motivation

- Connected to respect and responsibility

Montessori and Waldorf schools actually have *very structured* environments—just without shouting or shaming.

☑ Children learn to manage time, care for materials, resolve conflicts peacefully, and take ownership.

One teacher remarked, "In our classroom, silence isn't forced—it emerges because children are focused."

8. "Kids from alternative systems can't do well in competitive exams."

This depends on **timing and guidance**—not the system.

Many Montessori & Waldorf students from IB, IGCSE, and NIOS backgrounds have successfully cracked NEET, JEE, CLAT, and other competitive exams after focused preparation.

☑ These children often bring **conceptual clarity, time management, and resilience** to the table.

What matters is not the method, but when and how transition to exam prep is planned.

How to Spot a Myth

Ask yourself:

- Is this belief **based on fear or fact**?

- Has it been passed down without question?

- Have I seen real-life stories that **contradict** this idea?

Closing Thoughts

Don't let outdated assumptions stop you from giving your child a meaningful, joyful education.

The world is changing. Education is evolving.

And the child in front of you is **not a clone of you**—they are their own person, deserving an environment that honours their pace, their gifts, and their dreams.

Parent Prompt: Conversation Starter

"What's one belief about education that you've always had but now want to re-examine after reading this?"

Next Chapter Preview: Chapter 9 – Transitioning from Traditional to Alternative Schooling.

In the next chapter, we'll discuss how to help children (and parents!) move smoothly from conventional schooling to alternative systems—emotionally, academically, and socially.

Chapter 9:

Transitioning from Traditional to Alternative Schooling

"Growth begins at the edge of our comfort zones."
– Unknown

Shifting your child from a traditional school system to an alternative one can feel like moving countries—same child, new language, different rhythm. It takes **trust, planning, and patience**. But with the right approach, this transition can become a powerful growth journey for both you and your child.

Let's explore how.

1. Understanding the Emotional Shift

In traditional schools, children often get used to **external motivators**—marks, punishments, prizes, ranks.

In an alternative setup, those are replaced with:

- Intrinsic motivation

- Self-reflection

- Joyful learning

- Real-world responsibility

At first, some children may feel confused or even "bored" because there's no external push.

🔁 **Reframe it**: This isn't boredom—it's detox. After years of stress-based motivation, they're learning to **reconnect with curiosity**.

Real-life: 8-year-old Arjun, who moved from a CBSE school to a Waldorf system, kept asking for "homework" and "tests." His teacher gave him storytelling and movement-based math. Within a month, he was solving word problems in song and dance—*and loving it.*

2. Preparing Parents First

Often, it's not the child who struggles with the transition—it's the parent.

You may worry:

- *Is this system rigorous enough?*

- *Will my child fall behind?*

- *How will we face relatives, neighbours, society?*

☑ The best antidote to these fears is **research and real-life connection**. Visit the school. Observe classrooms. Talk to other parents. Track alumni stories.

Remember: You're not giving up structure. You're choosing **a different kind of structure**—one that values balance, wholeness, and real-world skills.

Tip: Keep a small journal of your own doubts, and revisit it every 3 months. You'll notice how many of them start to fade as you see your child thrive.

3. Supporting Your Child During the Switch

Here are practical tips to ease the transition:

🌱 a) Allow for an "unlearning" phase

Let your child decompress. Don't expect instant academic results. They may need to adjust from:

- Being passive recipients → to active participants

- Competing with others → to collaborating with peers

- Memorizing → to understanding

🧠 **b) Keep lines of communication open**

Ask open-ended questions like:

- "What surprised you today?"

- "What was the most fun?"

- "Anything you found tricky?"

This helps children process their shift emotionally.

📖 **c) Trust the process**

There may be days when your child says, "We just did   art   today."
But often, that art involves math, science, culture, and storytelling—all **hidden inside the joy**.

4. Academic Transitions

Contrary to fear, alternative schools **do have strong academic structures**. They're just less visible.

📑 Examples:

- In a Montessori class, a 7-year-old may be multiplying using bead chains, not worksheets.

- In a Waldorf school, a 10-year-old learns grammar through puppet plays and poetry.

The **key shift** is from rote recall to deep, contextual learning.

☑️ Tip for parents: Stay curious. Ask the school how concepts are taught. You'll be amazed at the depth, even without textbooks.

5. Handling Social Feedback

The most common external pressure is: **"What if your child can't cope later?"**

But here's what research and real-life say:

- Children who learn in stress-free, choice-driven environments **develop better mental health and motivation**

- Transitioning back into mainstream boards (if ever needed) is very possible—with the **right bridge years or coaching**

- Confidence, adaptability, and emotional resilience are the **strongest assets** for long-term success

Real-life: A 13-year-old from an IGCSE school in Pune transitioned to CBSE for NEET prep. With six months of orientation, he aced science concepts—because his **conceptual clarity** was already strong.

6. Building a Bridge at Home

You, as a parent, are the **anchor**. The home must support the school philosophy.

Here's how:

- Reduce emphasis on **marks and comparisons**

- Encourage **creative thinking and questions**

- Replace "Did you come first?" with "What did you learn today that made you think?"

- Prioritize **screen-free family time**, books, nature, and conversation

☑ Remember: Home and school are two wings of the same bird. If one wing flies in fear and the other in freedom, the child stays confused.

7. When Transitions Happen Late (Ages 10+)

While early transitions (ages 3–8) are easier, **later shifts can still be successful**.

Here's what to expect:

- Some initial resistance

- Social comparison ("My friends are in tuition and coaching")

- Academic mismatch (textbook vs project-based learning)

But with **counselling, peer support, and open discussions**, older children too begin to adapt. In fact, many later entrants become **leaders in alternative classrooms**—because they bring new perspectives.

Real-life: A 12-year-old girl in Bengaluru who joined a Montessori elementary after 6 years of CBSE said, "I was nervous at first. But here, I can *ask* questions. And they actually listen!"

8. Tracking Progress (Without Report Cards)

In alternative schools, traditional report cards are often replaced with:

- Portfolio reviews
- Learning journals
- Rubric-based teacher observations
- Student self-assessments
- Parent-teacher-child conferences

☑ These offer a **360-degree view** of the child—not just their scores, but their **skills, interests, and values**.

Ask your school for a sample report format. Keep personal notes of your child's growth in creativity, communication, kindness, and initiative.

Closing Thoughts

Transitioning out of conventional schooling isn't a rebellion—it's a realignment.

You are simply choosing a school where your child's **wonder, not just their marks**, matters.

Where learning is not about survival... but about *thriving*.

Stay the course. Trust the child. And let their love for learning lead the way.

Parent Prompt: Journal Exercise

"What fears do I have about transitioned schools? Which ones are based on facts? Which ones come from my own childhood experiences?"

Next Chapter Preview: Chapter 10 – The Role of Parents in Education Today

Coming up next, we dive deep into how the role of a 21st-century parent has shifted—from enforcer to enabler, from supervisor to co-learner. It's not just about choosing the right school—but about becoming the right learning partner.

Chapter 10:

The Role of Parents in Education Today

" Your child's first and most influential school is your home."

– Vinothkumar Subramanian

The world of education is changing rapidly. It's not just about the school anymore—it's about **what parents bring to the table**. In the past, parents were primarily seen as providers of financial support and caregivers. Today, they're learning partners, co-creators of a child's educational journey, and even advocates for the child's well-being.

Understanding the role parents now play in education is crucial, as this will empower you to guide your child through their learning path more effectively.

1. From Supervisor to Co-Learner

In the traditional school system, the parent's role often revolved around:

- Ensuring homework was done

- Enforcing study routines

- Monitoring grades and exam results

While this may have served its purpose, it fails to address the deeper, more meaningful learning process that alternative education systems emphasize.

In modern educational systems, particularly Montessori, Waldorf, and other progressive approaches, parents are seen as **co-learners**—partners in their child's intellectual and emotional development.

You're not just there to check assignments; you are part of the discovery process. This means **learning alongside** your child—engaging in their curiosities, questioning the world with them, and supporting their exploration.

Real-life: Arvind, a father from Chennai, initially struggled to understand the concept of **open-ended learning** in Montessori. But after engaging in his son's activities at home—building structures from wooden blocks and discussing their designs—he began to see how these small activities fostered creativity and critical thinking. His own mindset shifted from "fixing" homework to "enjoying" the learning process.

2. Building a Learning Environment at Home

Creating a **learning-rich environment** at home doesn't require expensive gadgets or fancy bookshelves. In fact, it's often about **simple practices** that foster curiosity, creativity, and critical thinking:

- **Provide diverse materials**: Natural objects (like stones, leaves, shells), open-ended toys, art supplies.

- **Encourage questions**: Answer "why" and "how" with curiosity, not as tasks to finish.

- **Facilitate meaningful conversations**: Discuss ideas, books, world events, and dreams over dinner.

- **Limit distractions**: Encourage reading and playtime that isn't interrupted by devices.

Your involvement helps **shape how your child sees the world**—not just as something to study, but as something to understand and engage with.

Tip: Create a special "learning corner" or "exploration zone" in your home. It could be a small corner with a globe, a collection of interesting books, or art materials. Let your child explore freely in this space.

3. Advocating for Your Child's Needs

Being involved in your child's education doesn't mean controlling every aspect—it's about **advocating for their unique needs**. This is especially important in alternative schooling systems, where each child's learning pace and method can vary.

Here's what advocating looks like:

- **Observing**: Watch how your child reacts to different activities and teaching methods.

- **Communicating**: Discuss your child's needs and progress with teachers regularly. Don't hesitate to ask for adjustments when needed.

- **Empowering**: Encourage your child to take ownership of their learning journey—ask them how they feel about the pace of learning and their interests.

Advocating means **recognizing your child's individuality** and making sure their needs—be it emotional, social, or intellectual—are met in the educational environment.

4. Emotional Support and Growth

In traditional education, academic success was often seen as the ultimate goal. But in alternative education systems, **emotional development** is just as important, if not more.

Children in progressive schools like Montessori or Waldorf schools are encouraged to **express themselves** emotionally, develop their **social skills**, and understand the world through **empathy and experience**.

As parents, you can **nurture emotional growth** by:

- **Validating their feelings**: Don't dismiss their emotional responses.

- **Encouraging expression**: Whether it's through art, dance, or conversation, encourage your child to share their feelings.

- **Modelling emotional resilience**: Show them how you handle stress, disappointment, and joy. Your actions speak louder than words.

When children are emotionally supported at home, they're more confident in navigating the challenges they face at school and in the world beyond.

Real-life: Neha, a mother from Hyderabad, found that her daughter's performance in school improved dramatically when she began acknowledging her daughter's frustrations and offering solutions. Rather than just pushing her to study more, she allowed her daughter to work at her own pace and provided support where necessary.

5. Managing Social Pressures and Peer Comparison

In today's competitive world, there's a lot of pressure on children to **fit in** with their peers. Parents can help their child **manage social pressures** by:

- **Teaching resilience**: Let them know it's okay to be different.

- **Fostering a growth mindset**: Encourage your child to see setbacks as learning opportunities.

- **Celebrating uniqueness**: Support their interests, even if they differ from the crowd.

When you model this attitude, your child learns not only how to handle peer pressure but also how to **stay true to themselves**. They'll be equipped to deal with challenges, whether they come from friends, family, or society.

6. Parents as Advocates of Change

Being part of an alternative educational system also means you can become an **advocate for change**—both within your community and the larger educational ecosystem. You'll become aware of the **limitations of conventional schooling** and see the **potential for reform** in how we educate our children.

This advocacy doesn't always have to be dramatic. It can begin in small ways:

- **Support your child's school**: Be an active member of the parent-teacher association (PTA).

- **Raise awareness**: Talk to friends and family about the benefits of alternative education.

- **Engage with policymakers**: Support movements that aim to make education more personalized and inclusive.

When you take an active role in transforming education for your child, you're contributing to a larger movement—one that believes in the potential of every child and the power of **educational diversity**.

7. Staying Open to Change

As education evolves, so does the role of the parent. Today's **parents need to be agile, open-minded, and willing to change** alongside their child's educational journey.

In a world where careers may shift, new technologies emerge, and societal values change, the skills your child needs most are adaptability, creativity, and emotional intelligence. Parents who embrace these same qualities create a **strong foundation** for their children.

Real-life: Rajesh and Priya, parents from Kolkata, made the conscious choice to support their son's transition from a traditional school to a progressive one. They were initially sceptical, but over time, they realized how this shift equipped their son with **problem-solving skills** and a love for learning. Their support helped him thrive in a world that constantly demands change.

Closing Thoughts

Being an involved parent doesn't mean controlling your child's education; it means being an **active participant** in their learning journey. It's about **empowering them** to explore, make mistakes, learn, and grow with your guidance—not your direction.

The world of education is in flux, and as parents, you are not just bystanders. You are co-pilots, advocates, and partners in shaping the future. Together, you and your child can redefine what it means to learn.

Parent Prompt: Journal Exercise

"What kind of parent do I want to be in my child's learning journey? How can I better support their emotional, intellectual, and social development?"

Next Chapter Preview: Chapter 11 – Exploring the Future of Education

In the final chapter, we take a glimpse into the future of education. What will schools look like 10 years from now? How can we best prepare our children for an ever-changing world? Stay tuned as we explore **education for the future**.

Chapter 11:

Exploring the Future of Education

*"The future belongs to those who learn, unlearn,
and relearn with wonder."*

– Alvin Toffler

As we stand at the intersection of the present and the future, **education** is one of the areas undergoing the most significant transformations. The future of education is no longer just about textbooks, exams, and classrooms—it's about **innovation**, **personalization**, and **preparing children for an uncertain world**. In this chapter, we explore how education is evolving and what it means for our children.

1. The Shift from Rote Learning to Critical Thinking

For centuries, education in India (and globally) has focused on **rote memorization**—students were expected to memorize and regurgitate information. While this method has its merits, especially in subjects like history or geography, it doesn't always encourage **deep understanding** or the development of critical thinking skills.

The future of education, however, emphasizes **problem-solving**, **creativity**, and the ability to think critically about the world around us. Students will no longer be asked to simply memorize facts; they will be **challenged to question** those facts, analyse information, and form their own conclusions.

For example, in **Montessori schools**, children are taught to **think independently**, ask questions, and **explore concepts on their own**. This helps them build strong problem-solving skills, which are essential for the future.

Real-life: In a Montessori school in Bangalore, students don't just read about historical events—they **simulate** those events, create debates, and analyze them through multiple perspectives. This process encourages them to think critically about what they read and to apply that knowledge in real-world scenarios.

2. The Integration of Technology in Education

The influence of technology on education is undeniable. From **digital classrooms** to **online learning platforms**, technology is reshaping how children learn, and how teachers deliver content. **Artificial intelligence (AI)** and **virtual reality (VR)** are becoming common tools in the classroom, offering immersive and personalized learning experiences.

In the future, children might be using **VR headsets** to explore the history of ancient civilizations, learning about **physics** through interactive simulations, or using **AI-powered tutors** that cater to their individual learning styles. This **customization** of learning allows children to **progress at their own pace**, focusing on areas they find challenging, and speeding through topics they grasp easily.

Real-life: Neha's daughter, a student at a school in Pune, has been using a **VR system** to learn about ecosystems. She has virtually "visited" rainforests, coral reefs, and the Arctic, interacting with creatures and environments she only knew through textbooks. This immersive learning experience has sparked her curiosity and encouraged her to learn more about science.

3. The Rise of Personalized Learning

The one-size-fits-all model of education is slowly becoming outdated. **Personalized learning**, which tailors the educational experience to each child's **learning style**, **pace**, and **interests**, is gaining traction. In this approach, students don't just follow a rigid curriculum—they take charge of their own learning journey, often with the help of teachers and digital tools.

In the future, we may see more **project-based learning**, where students choose projects that interest them and learn through hands-on experience. This **personalization** ensures that every child can **excel in their own way**, whether they are visual learners, auditory learners, or kinaesthetic learners.

Real-life: Raghav's son, a student at an international school, chose to explore **renewable energy** for his science project. Instead of following a pre-designed path, he **designed his own experiments**, researched various energy sources, and even built a small solar panel to demonstrate his findings. His teacher guided him through the process, but the initiative was all his.

4. A Focus on Soft Skills and Emotional Intelligence

As automation and AI continue to grow, **soft skills** like **creativity**, **communication**, and **emotional intelligence (EQ)** are becoming increasingly important. These skills are things that machines can't replicate, and they're critical in helping children succeed in both their personal and professional lives.

In the future, education systems will place a **stronger emphasis on emotional intelligence**, teaching children not only how to excel academically but also how to understand and manage their emotions, build **relationships**, and collaborate effectively with others.

Real-life: In a Waldorf school in Delhi, children participate in activities that build **empathy** and **collaboration**—such as **group projects**, **arts** that require team effort, and **storytelling** that encourages children to express emotions. These activities foster strong **emotional intelligence**, which will serve them well in life.

5. Globalization and Cultural Awareness

As the world becomes increasingly interconnected, education will need to prepare children for **global citizenship**. In the future, children won't just be learning about their local culture—they'll be learning about cultures, traditions, and **global issues** that affect people all over the world.

Cultural awareness and **global collaboration** will be integral to the curriculum. Children will learn how to **communicate across cultures**, work with people from diverse backgrounds, and tackle challenges that require a **global perspective**.

Real-life: In an IB school in Mumbai, students frequently participate in **Model United Nations (MUN)** conferences, where they represent different countries and engage in debates on international issues. This encourages them to view the world through different lenses and helps them understand the complexities of global challenges.

6. Flexible Learning Pathways

The traditional path of going from school to college to career is no longer the only route to success. The future of education will offer **more flexible learning pathways**—from apprenticeships and vocational training to online certifications and micro-credentials. This allows children to **choose their path** based on their interests and career goals, instead of being forced into a rigid academic track.

In this environment, children will have the **freedom to explore different careers** and education systems that align with their passions, enabling them to grow into well-rounded, adaptable individuals.

Real-life: Arjun, a teenager from Kochi, is interested in **graphic design**. While attending high school, he has also enrolled in an online **graphic design course**. This combination of alternative schooling and specialized online learning gives him the skills he needs for his future career in a way that a traditional schools might not have.

Chapter 12:

Making the Right Choice – Selecting the Best School for Your Child

"Choosing a school is not about finding the best place — it's about finding the right place for your child's soul to bloom."

– Vinothkumar Subramanian

Selecting a school is one of the most important decisions parents will make for their children. This decision not only impacts their **academic growth** but also their **personal development**, social skills, and future opportunities. With so many options available in India, ranging from traditional to alternative educational systems, it's crucial to approach this decision with careful thought and consideration.

In this chapter, we will guide you through the **steps to selecting the right school**, considering all the aspects we've discussed in the previous chapters.

1. Understanding Your Child's Needs

Before diving into the process of school selection, it is essential to understand your child's **learning style**, **interests**, and **personality**. Every child is unique, and what works for one might not work for another. Some children thrive in traditional classrooms, while others might do better in more **innovative** or **hands-on** learning environments.

Ask yourself the following questions:

- Does my child prefer structure or flexibility?

- Is my child more independent or do they need guidance?

- What are my child's interests? Do they enjoy creative activities like arts and crafts or are they more inclined towards scientific exploration?

- How does my child react to challenges? Are they more comfortable with gentle encouragement or do they enjoy a competitive environment?

Answering these questions will help you identify which educational approach aligns with your child's natural tendencies and needs. It will also allow you to assess if a particular school's philosophy and approach would be a good fit.

2. Aligning with Your Educational Goals

Every parent has a vision for their child's education. Some parents focus on **academic excellence**, while others prioritize **emotional development** or **holistic growth**. Some value schools with a strong emphasis on **sports**, **arts**, or **technology**, while others want schools that focus on **character building** and **life skills**.

When selecting a school, it's essential to ask yourself:

- What are my long-term educational goals for my child?

- Do I want my child to follow a traditional or alternative educational path?

- How important are extracurricular activities (sports, music, drama, etc.) in my decision-making?

- Do I want my child to develop a strong academic foundation, or are character development and life skills equally important?

By clarifying your priorities, you'll be able to choose a school that aligns with both your child's needs and your educational goals for them.

3. Investigating School Methods and Philosophies

Now that you understand your child's needs and your goals, it's time to explore the methods and philosophies offered by various schools. Whether you choose **Montessori**, **Waldorf**, **CBSE**, **ICSE**, **IB**, or another system, each offers distinct advantages and drawbacks.

For example, a **Montessori school** offers a child-centred learning environment that nurtures **independence** and **creativity**, making it an excellent choice for children who benefit from self-directed learning. However, if you're looking for a more structured, exam-oriented approach, a **CBSE** or **ICSE** school might be a better fit.

When considering the school's philosophy, here are some questions to ask:

- Does the school focus on **individualized learning** or a **one-size-fits-all approach**?

- What is the school's **teaching methodology**? Is it based on hands-on learning, project-based activities, or traditional teaching methods?

- Does the school integrate **technology** into its curriculum? If yes, to what extent?

- How does the school support **emotional and social development**?

- What is the student-teacher ratio? Does the school maintain small class sizes to ensure personalized attention?

These questions will help you understand how the school's approach fits your child's needs and your educational philosophy.

4. Examining School Facilities and Extracurricular Offerings

The physical environment and extracurricular activities offered by a school can significantly influence your child's overall experience. A school's **facilities**—from classrooms and playgrounds to technology resources—can either enhance or hinder learning.

Some points to consider include:

- Does the school have **modern classrooms**, **science labs**, and **technology** for interactive learning?

- Are there **outdoor play areas** and **sports facilities** that encourage physical activity and teamwork?

- What extracurricular activities (sports, arts, drama, music, etc.) are offered to help children develop their talents?

- How does the school support **special needs** or offer **remedial support** for students who need additional help?

Although not all schools have extensive resources, a school that offers a rich variety of **extracurricular activities** and an environment conducive to both **learning** and **play** can significantly enrich your child's development.

5. Checking the School's Reputation and Reviews

Word of mouth and online reviews can provide valuable insights into a school's reputation. Speak to other parents and alumni to get a sense of their experiences. **Parent testimonials** can reveal how the school deals with challenges like bullying, student welfare, and academic pressure.

Additionally, investigate if the school has been recognized for excellence in any area, such as **curriculum quality, teacher training**, or **student outcomes**.

Some ways to gather information about a school's reputation:

- Talk to **current students** and their parents about their experiences.

- Read **online reviews** and testimonials.

This feedback will help you get a clearer picture of the school's strengths and weaknesses.

6. Considering the Location and Affordability

The location of the school plays an important role in your decision. A **school close to home** will make commuting easier for both you and your child. Consider the following:

- Is the school easily accessible? What is the transportation like?

- Does the school provide **transportation services**? If so, what is the route and cost?

- Is the school **affordable**, considering your budget and long-term financial commitments?

Choosing a school that is **conveniently located** and fits within your budget will reduce logistical stress and allow you to focus on your child's education.

7. Visiting the School

Finally, visit the schools you're considering. A **personal visit** will allow you to see the school environment firsthand, interact with the teachers, and understand the overall vibe of the school.

Some things to observe during your visit:

- Is the school environment **welcoming** and **nurturing**?

- How do the teachers interact with the students? Do they seem engaged and attentive?

- Are the facilities clean, safe, and well-maintained?

- Does the school have a **positive atmosphere**, where students appear happy and motivated?

A visit will give you a deeper understanding of the school's culture and whether it aligns with your expectations.

Conclusion

Choosing a school is a complex but rewarding process. By understanding your child's needs, aligning your goals with the school's philosophy, and carefully assessing all aspects of the institution, you'll make an informed decision that supports your child's growth and development.

In the world of education, there is no one-size-fits-all answer. But with the right approach and careful consideration, you can find a school that will help your child **thrive**, **learn**, and **succeed**.

Final Thought: The school you choose today will help shape the future your child will inherit tomorrow. Choose wisely, and they will flourish!

End of Book

This concludes the guide on *"Selecting a School!"*. Thank you for reading and taking the time to explore the complex yet fascinating world of education. May your journey in choosing the best school for your child be filled with thoughtful decisions and future success.

Psychometric Test: Discover Your Child's Ideal Schooling Path

Instructions:

- For each statement, mark the option that best represents your belief.

- Be honest — there are no right or wrong answers!

Options:

- A) Strongly Agree

- B) Agree

- C) Disagree

- D) Strongly Disagree

Questions:

1. I want my child to do independent projects without too much adult guidance.

2. I prefer a highly structured curriculum with clear goals over flexible exploration.

3. I believe traditional exams and rankings are important for my child's growth.

4. I value creativity and original thinking more than memorization and academic grades.

5. I would rather have my child assessed on skills and personality growth than exam marks.

6. I believe fewer exams and more continuous assessment will benefit children better.

7. I want my child to have international exposure and global learning opportunities.

8. I prefer a school that has strong acceptance among Indian colleges and traditional boards.

9. I believe education should focus on the whole child: emotional, social, and academic.

10. I think discipline, deadlines, and competition help build character in students.

11. I would prefer my child to learn at their own pace rather than be compared against others.

12. I believe in flexible learning paths instead of one-size-fits-all teaching.

13. I would like my child to have access to international curriculums like IB or IGCSE.

14. I am comfortable considering open or alternative schooling paths for my child.

15. I believe emotional well-being is as important as academic performance.

Scoring Instructions:

- **For Questions favouring Alternative/International approach**
  (Q1, Q4, Q5, Q6, Q7, Q9, Q11, Q12, Q13, Q14, Q15):
    - **A) Strongly Agree = 4 points**
    - **B) Agree = 3 points**
    - **C) Disagree = 2 points**
    - **D) Strongly Disagree = 1 point**
- **For Questions favoring Traditional approach**
  (Q2, Q3, Q8, Q10):
    - **A) Strongly Agree = 1 point**
    - **B) Agree = 2 points**
    - **C) Disagree = 3 points**
    - **D) Strongly Disagree = 4 points**

Result Interpretation:

Total Score	Interpretation
55 – 60	Strong fit for Alternative/International (Montessori, Waldorf, KFI, IB, IGCSE)

45 – 54	⚡ Balanced fit: Can adapt to progressive CBSE/ICSE schools or international curricula
30 – 44	⚫ Best suited for Traditional Schools (CBSE/ICSE with structured methods)
Below 30	⚫ Highly Conventional: Traditional State Boards / Old-style CBSE strongly recommended

---

Quick Example Scoring:

Suppose you answer:

- Strongly Agree to Q1 (4 points)

- Strongly Agree to Q2 (1 point)

- Agree to Q3 (2 points)
  and so on...

You will sum up all your points to find where you land!

🎯 Closing Tip for Readers:

"There is no *good* or *bad* schooling system. The right school is the one that aligns with your child's personality, dreams, and your family's core values."

References & Recommended Reading

Educational Philosophies and Systems

- Montessori, Maria. *The Absorbent Mind*. Holt Paperbacks.

- Steiner, Rudolf. *The Education of the Child*. Anthroposophical Press.

- Krishnamurti, Jiddu. *Education and the Significance of Life*. HarperCollins.

- Dewey, John. *Democracy and Education*. The Free Press.

- Tagore, Rabindranath. *Creative Unity*. Macmillan.

- Holt, John. *How Children Learn*. Da Capo Press.

- Piaget, Jean. *The Psychology of the Child*. Basic Books.

Modern Schooling and Curriculum Studies

- Zhao, Yong. *World Class Learners: Educating Creative and Entrepreneurial Students*. Corwin Press.

- Robinson, Ken. *Creative Schools: The Grassroots Revolution That's Transforming Education*. Viking.

- Mitra, Sugata. *The Hole in the Wall: Self-Organizing Systems in Education*. TED Books.

Understanding Indian Education Boards

- CBSE Curriculum Documents (Available at cbse.gov.in)

- CISCE Guidelines for ICSE and ISC Boards (Available at cisce.org)

- Cambridge International Education Curriculum Guides (Available at cambridgeinternational.org)

- International Baccalaureate Organization Publications (Available at ibo.org)

  - National Institute of Open Schooling Resources (Available at nios.ac.in)